POETS OF QUEENS 2
ANTHOLOGY

POETS OF QUEENS 2
ANTHOLOGY

Edited by Jared Beloff and Olena Jennings

Poets of Queens Press
New York, 2024

Designed and composed by Oleksandr Fraze-Frazenko.

ISBN: 979-8-9904733-1-7

Contents

Sherese Francis

NDIGITALE: SUPERPOSITION OF THE GREEN AND THE INDUSTRIAL PARK AND ... (WHAT IF WILSON RANTUS WAS A GEOLOGIST?)

> *Most of the property on the grounds of the Green has been industrialized, although there is one lot that may have the remains of a structural foundation of a building from the era. — Noah Sheidlower from Untapped Cities Article, "The Green, A Forgotten African American Community in Jamaica, Queens*

Will the ground remember you?

When searching the internet for history of Jamaica,
Whose name will show up in the results?

The Green? A farm?
A Black community?
1830? Jamaica, Queens?
Did you know slavery existed in New York?
Douglass St. and Liberty Ave?
Between 168th Street and 175th Street?

Passing by a lot while riding the Q83;
It was always there in my sight:
Found embedded in junk cars, auto repair shops,
Gatemakers, butchers, railroad tracks,
A strip mall, and York college —
Out of place and out of time,
Overgrown with vines, grass, graffiti,
Revolting against pavement.

What can be remembered in a place forgotten?

The architects of the city crumble the past into ruins.
Take the sand to use for a new profitable construction.
The concrete shifts around and what was once known

Is now a memory — the promise of industry.
Structures falling and rising up and
Places entered before for nourishment—
Green Farm Supermarket,
King's Fish Market —the doors are now closed.

The bus terminal is moving.
The LIRR no longer goes directly to Brooklyn
From where I live.

Does a presence hinder development?
Is the carving of memory
Into stone a hindrance
To evolution?
Is legal a safe passage?
The law won't help;
Others are coming in
To claim this space;
Treating you like a ghost
Haunting what you once called home.

How to hold on when one reality begins to fade into another?
Will I still be welcomed?
Was I ever welcomed?

Wilson Rantus began a petition
For his Black community to receive suffrage;
Organized a conference of broken bones and pots.
Rantus whispers into each shard:
I pray we move towards a right to freedom
Like roots pushing through the cracks of concrete
Against the burial of wilderness;
Like a weed in the gears of industry;
Like John Jefferson pelting stones
At a structure of violence.

The Avenue has a church on almost every block:
Valencia, First Presbyterian, Grace, First Reformed Dutch.
I am still searching for a sustainable and close-knit community.
I fear the hostilities and indifference of privilege —
A new hotel, a new luxury apartment show up in the neighborhood.

First Presbyterian once housed a free school.
Rantus dreamed of a free Black school that never came
Or didn't last.

Does the ground remember his dream?

Rantus' marble gravestone reappeared
By a fence in the backyard of a Queens college professor.
A geologist.
A boulder now sits on the campus in honor of him.
The boulder is a billion-year-old gneiss.
I am told it is to remember some changes are slow.

What would be found if I searched the archives
for The Anglo-African? Or The Colored American?
If I searched for Thomas Hamilton?
Would I hear the roar breaking from underground?

Does the ground still remember?

Rantus and his family were reburied in an unmarked grave
In Evergreen.
History layered over and over;
History structuring our nows without a name.

What story does the boulder tell?
If I searched it, would it give me a result I am looking for?
Explain the processes of change over time?
The shifts on the streets where I walk?

Am I integrating
into a dying machine?
Do memories reprogram the earth?
What will the fossil records say?

What will the ground remember of my presence?

Maria Lisella

PROGRESS

He spoke philosophy over binary
numbers: *to be poor in America is a sin,*
to be in debt is the American way.

A wounded WWII vet who never owed
a dime – did that make him unpatriotic?
Poor, we were close to, but did not notice;

not the pharmacist, not the school
where my mother bartered for tuition
by sewing the nuns' habits. No one

noticed. *Someday no one will pay*
with money. Clerks at the Colombian
café cluck as Millennials try to pay
$1.35 for *café con leche* with plastic.

No aceptamos plástico aquí, buenos días.

IT'S ALL ABOUT THE COMPANY

Bellerose, 2011

I said I'd stay with her
for the hurricane
diminished to a tropical storm.

No one had to tell the birds
to take cover on her patio
slipping between empty coffee cans.

Emerging to nibble on stale breadcrumbs
Squeezed back into the tunnel of cans
A row of them tucked under the eave

Positioned to keep them
from creating nests.
Gave them sanctuary instead.

The storm rolled in.
Whipped the white birch into switches
Snapping at the gutters 'til morning.

2.
I kept her company
during the storm. She
was unafraid, at 92,
not much scares her
but she loves company,
stormy weather,
heat waves, ice storms,
It's all about the company.

Trace Howard DePass

[#NEWPIC] TWEET OF BAISLEY POND, QUEENS, WHERE THE CRANE INSISTS THE BODIES IN IT ← ARE BLACK!!

ain't no mother ain't   no savior here but

made your boy human

in brief forgiveness   down years, books, in which

ain't none of us looked

one in one gone eye   one near ponds cranes (& swan graze

perched at ebbed-most {ebony}

knees, yes the race   in lakes, tanks, is black {human}

but shot down as bird

splattered thru abstract   felled as Orion's whole pant leg

in it, except here i mother the crane

with which nothing flies   cause they ain't, are dust

, and you stare as i stare for so long that:

wild shit! {day flaps}   my feather-plop against wretched

air and this wet cement numbed by fishbone

i evade. but bound: bird: i... "crane", so well

so high i touch "white",

faux-foe forreal white   just a bit *in front, afraid, of me*

i touch again and nothing, wed

i feel nothing, won   white like swan; song; son

-der as rain relents for ALL: bin or bid

like sneaker to game   the sneaker wire hangs

until it fills us up so much the pond

barrels read 23,   contains HOMIES

where oil was contained, here its fossil

fuels, O, this black this   veiled beneath black → *that*

was somebody's everything, all there is,

all they is. all they is.   ain't no baby ain't   is

love, *a hard thing, harder before tender*   *out here*

i she YOU as we

barely love in-love   barely love this world

in the big improv *[we be playin]*

can't write it all down   barely speak a new

but must and perhaps

yes *might* might just make   me, Black as not much,

m(in)e *[mine in me]* as beak thru birdseye, into loving

someone, as warm as   gods tethered wounds, *here*

seared, the heart race be

-tween wood & city,   the heart bound well to

Abandon, *[should-&-pity,]* the interim-libation,

its run-on hyphen   before gods' journeys'

dark eve had begun

milking the #Dogon,   before yolk unbound

and #Gnostics of #SouthSide *suggest* #DayDreams

dreamt us, UP, FAM, bound-   dead, but was. *dead-born* [#Dead-Ass....

against #NotLiving, Living, against me

-mory, against… & against…   , cue → queue → of *sirens*]

Robert Kaplan

BOWNE PARK

Flushing, NY 11354

When I was a lad of single digits
Bowne Park was the place to be:
4 blocks long, 1 block wide, 1 block away;
always, I and other kids on the block,
when we weren't running through backyards
or running bases on sidewalks
or board games in a basement on a rainy day
off we would go,
sometimes with parents
always with blessings
always well-supplied for whatever adventures lay ahead.

Bowne Park had everything:
a pond with carp for fishing,
turtles sunning on rocks smartly out of reach,
minnows bending and curving in watery ripples of spotted light.
Sometimes we would grab our rods
pack slices of supermarket bread in special plastic bags
and sit cross-legged on the concrete edge of the pond
rods and packages scattered around us,
we would tear small pieces of bread from the soft inside
roll them into doughy balls
then sink our hooks deep deep in
hidden from unsuspecting fish with mouths open wide.

Still, when we threw our lines into the water usually nothing
    happened
so when there was a tug it was that much more exciting:
oh, how we would yell and scream and cheer, all of us,
it didn't matter who had caught it,
it was the biggest fish, always,
so of course we had to yell even more if it was reeled in,
jumping in and out of the water toward us
and then as it flipped and flopped on the concrete edge.

Sadly, we always threw it back,
even though we all wanted pets.
Probably one of us had been yelled at by parents
who were presented with a plastic bag filled with scummy pond
    water
and a grimy miserable fish.
It was part of the ritual:
whoever caught it would grab its slimy undulating body,
unhook its slimy undulating mouth,
the rest of us yelling and screaming
even kids from elsewhere who we didn't know
they would suddenly appear and yell and scream too,
and only when the fish was thrown back in
and flipped itself rapidly below that murky surface,
only then would they wander away.

Other times we would just sit on the edge
concrete warm on our bottoms from hours of sun,
we would dangle our legs over the water
and watch the turtles paddle, slowly and deliberately,
always with purpose,
always just out of reach:
another rock to sun on, dipping under for food.
They never got close even though sometimes we would try.
Sometimes we would fall in.

It was a great pond for falling in.
It was a great park for falling in.
Riding our bikes along paths that circled within and around,
paths that swirled further away, deep into the trees,
paths along which single-digit me
could ride round and through,
breeze on my skin, soft sigh of the leaves,
until the shouts of someone when I came too close
because attention I certainly was not paying,
only to stay away from the playground at the far end
where the bad kids hung out.
Truth be told, they weren't bad at all,
just a bit older, a bit rough and tumble,
and that's not bad, that's just a bit different.

Also too there was a hill for winter sleighing,
it sloped right down to the pond
and sometimes we just couldn't stop so right in we would go,
into the icy water laughing and yelling all the way to the end.
But the best was when there was rickety ice covered with snow
and our sleighs just kept going and bouncing
and ploughed as far as they could.
Sometimes there even was ice skating.
Oh, those pre-climate change winters when it got and stayed cold
for more than two days at a time.

This is not just nostalgia.

For I don't know how long prior my mother had been looking at houses,
the apartment in Fresh Meadows two bedrooms
but still crowded with children
and my father's mother nearby needing more care.
Amazingly this one checked every box:
a bedroom for them
one for my sister
one for my slightly older brother and me,
two full bathrooms and a basement with a full kitchen
for my father's mother who kept kosher
which we most certainly did not,
even a sun room where she could sit and watch the world go by
and where at night she would sleep.
The front entrance faced the driveway
so we could run outside and my mother didn't have to be so concerned.
My brother was excited because the park was so close
which meant he had a place to keep his cattle.

Years later my mother told me that when she first saw the house
    she rang the neighbor's bell
and discovered that they, too, had 3 children,
almost the same age.
The deal was sealed.
Shortly after my 5th birthday and shortly before my sister's 2nd is
    when we moved in
but shortly before then we took a field trip.
I'm not still sure why
nor do I recollect how we got there,

but with 3 kids and a stroller, taxi is most likely,
the 2 buses too many ways for things to go wrong.
The house was empty and locked.
But the backyard was open
and the water hook-up for the hose had been turned on.
Around the corner was a small grocery store
and I remember that we held hands as we walked
and we bought a package of small dixie cups and a loaf of
    Wonder Bread
and we sat in a circle on the flagstone patio and drank small cups of water
and made small balls of dough from the slices of bread
and we ate those too.

At some point the kids from next door came over and we all ate
    and drank and played.
Certainly it's possible that my mother had called beforehand
to let them know we were coming
and to extend an invitation.
Certainly it would have been the neighborly thing to do but also,
how else would we have gone to the bathroom?
We were young, the house was locked,
so perhaps an early good neighbor exchange:
bathroom for me, Wonder Bread and water for thee.
It was just the beginning.
Kids all over the block and Bowne Park, always Bowne Park.
Even when I switched elementary schools and lost all my other friends
still there was the park and kids on the block.

As we got older, fishing and bike riding became touch football
in the small field right by the pond
but really, that was the only change.
Even when junior high school started
and I sensed I was different and some of the kids in school did too,
especially one boy in 8th grade,
still, there was the park and kids on the block.

Now it's years later, 64 of them to be exact since that day we moved in,
and I'm at the other end of my life,
wandering away like the other kids
but unlike them, not just for a visit, wandering back.
Whenever we would bump into each other, how different it was,

18

and yet none of that mattered.
And the parents, some of them remained.
And Bowne Park, it remained.

The first time I returned to New York I lived in Manhattan
and my parents would come in for a concert or a show
and sometimes I would meet them and we would laugh and
    enjoy.
Always there was a good meal.
Always there was wine.
Sometimes I would come out to the house and do odd things that
    needed doing
and my father would talk about his book collection and my
    mother about her teaching.
Always there was wine.
Always there was a good meal.
I would tell them some of what I was up to,
not everything, of course, but that's okay.

Then it was my parents' turn.
First my father, after he retired and before my mother did,
he would walk the one block over, settle himself on a bench
next to the field, overlooking the pond.
He would look at the children and the geese and the sky
and the trees and the water rippling in light.
It gave him such solace.
He loafed and invited his soul.
Sometimes I would walk with him
and of course it was different but in a way it was not.

The second time I returned to New York I again lived in Manhattan.
My father could no longer walk to the park by himself
so sometimes my mother, now retired, would go with him
and sometimes it was me,
coming out to the house more and more:
the clop clop of his cane in one hand and holding my arm with the other
and we would sit on that same bench and we would watch.
Sometimes we would walk to the bocci courts next to the
    playground,
at the far end of the park.
Neither of us knew the rules but still,

the exactness of it, the way they would line up the balls.
We could sit for a long time and sometimes we did.

Even though some parents moved away
still there were holdouts, mine and a few others,
they loved their homes and the neighborhood and the park.
Some of them died there,
a few others and mine.

One fall, a few months before my father passed away,
the Bowne Park Civic Association sponsored a concert
and our neighbor across the street, now deceased, then president,
took a picture of him in a wheelchair,
my mother and I standing behind, all of us grinning from ear to ear
and, suddenly, there we were, on the front cover of the newsletter,
memorialized forever in slanting light.
I was staying overnight half the week
because, in the mist of his sundowning,
I was the one person with whom he was always calm.

Then I was out at the house to be with my mother.
When she was in the mood, together we would walk to the park
and we would sit on a bench and we would watch and reminisce.
It was funny and sad, both, and we would laugh and our eyes
    would shine in the sun.
Sometimes we would walk to the bocci courts at the far end of
    the park
and we would sit and we would watch.
The people were different but it was very much the same:
the exactness of it, the way they would line up the balls.
Sometimes I would escort our neighbor across the street
and we'd have a cookout in the backyard,
just the 3 of us, the 3 holdouts.
Sometimes my mother would walk to the park by herself,
the green and the open spaces and the little kiddies running around.
It was a new immigration wave but she didn't care.
She had an open heart. She knew that immigration had saved her life.
The kiddies were cute and she loved to watch.

Even when I moved in full-time and we settled into the rhythm
of rooms and outings and meals that still I miss so,
still when I wasn't around, still Bowne Park was right there.
She would walk the one block
or talk on the phone with friends
and when I wasn't at work
I would drive her to visit and they would talk and reminisce.
It was almost always the wives who remained.
They all had known me since I was yay big
and now here I was, the one who had returned.
Yes, for my mother they were very happy,
and yes, while they wouldn't admit it,
by their occasional comments I could tell they were a bit jealous too.

Now I walk to Bowne Park and it's still the same winding paths
and the fields where I played ball with the other kids
and the pond where I went fishing and which I fell into and rode
    my bike around
and the hill that we used to sleigh down when it snowed.
The pond rarely freezes over anymore but still there are families
    and little kids
and everyone enjoys it so.

I'm not sure I do now but that's probably more about me.
I see single-digit me running around, having a blast,
but of course I'm long past single digits,
an adult gay man ensconced in a neighborhood
where at least on the surface I've seen no one like me.
I keep wondering how a place so comfortable
can be such a marker of how I no longer belong,
people doing what I used to do oh so many years ago
and still I know every corner and every nook.

In fact, sometimes I wonder why I'm still here but really, I know
    the answer.
There's a house to unwind, if I want to,
which sometimes I do and usually I don't:
it's my home, after all,
it's my life almost my entire life.
But I don't have to make that decision,
not now, maybe never,

my mother's ongoing gift for all those years,
for the 3 of us, for the 2 of us,
for 1.
Even now she stretches herself across the ineffable
to remind me that I can, eventually,
perhaps, create a new life, right here if I so choose.

But when I'm in Bowne Park it's my whole life,
beckoning me in its strange familiarity.
Yes, there are now turtle sculptures
and a little free library
and the playground has been redone, as have the bocci courts,
and the pond has been dredged and redredged more times than I
    can remember.
But it's like the rest of the neighborhood:
there are teardowns and McMansions
but mostly it's houses from 64 years ago
and even the trees and so much the same.

Even in winter, when it's not too cold,
sometimes I go for a walk, just to get out of the house,
or in the summer, when I don't want to be in the backyard,
when I want to see people
even though there's no one I know.

Each year Bowne Park remains.
Whether I'm here or not
whether I am or not,
each year it remains.

Paolo Javier

STUDYING ROSES IN TENTH DIMENSION

for Paul Mpagi Sepuya

there's you me Karnika near Route 9 wave to Baby feet I tear not the Still would said been around should for have open sea I love Anything man want I of like frame within frame rectangle & Stand else know sky I remember your Through teeth clenched & need to square black&white color the artist in & to my refuse In my 5'6 Wil E. 5'6 Wil E. Coyote will settle or don't my fly right sky seen poesy encounters me the by finger buried in a flowerpot in paired love death the mouse feelings youth shared ever only Then shared their studio wounded, practicing Oh for not the faux imperialist gaze of taken come from find I I camera toy tongue justice aloud the bayou phallus facing youth image of I mind much dream so I'm with the farmer's head TGIFrieda Kahlo! Head TGIFrieda Kahlo! With soul PAUL MPAGE SEPUYA Now hands of Brown to can the parts You private like assembled of jeans & white sneakers kiss no-face broken disappointment outcast from image Of I remember one hundred passport hairstyles yr legs against white wood in parts Einsehen green X in blue gaze through persona docket cozying by away thing cloud Just that so In the original manner Near all for there's Could youth yearlong head fire Two lower torso hinges In imperialist gaze of 3 major races ever set foot in Not the rain drenched flower in hand of When I remember my left pinky the Wil which above Santos lemongrass apart negotiate the bunnies drinking sugar Why did my eyes locate years Eva O Frame assembled from square appear in fragments First Humpty dumpty shorn Paolo to his in name there is no self portrait in Ever been Your the please do week have galaxy saw a baby we Our Thee me for see urge to Drawbridge talk all of previous to Rose land to train me but FUCK YOU BIG BROTHER fair Innie, outie I of the images assembled in part Stillness & class Dosido to the carving knife collective gaze on an all-knowing white isolation How many squares in this Beautiful bare ass Pectoral calves To No, take a walk then past I And I dreams of that's Anna May Minute neighborhoods a selves Beijing Was could With swollen thoroughfare That pull me apart limb by emptiness nd by as Not the for When I make poetry They PORTRAIT Poem finally sung to by plural Past Friday In I I'm limb reel come around the mountain gathered flower the savor of family Done been light insistent Dont put em back together

Ananda Lima

PHOTOGRAPH: QUEENSBOROUGH

Bridge and forget
the rest of your name
the water
below still
satin black
moonlight silver
soundless shutter
and the shuffle
of pedestrians
electric
bikes on your right and
the cars: waves and heart
over bump
soundless
in the picture
suck the moon in
suck the city into screen
the bright beyond
hold it in HDR and long
exposure, the city
sits in between
open curtains
cupped
in the palms of your hands

Bruce E. Whitacre

QUEENS HAIKU

Long bakery wait
Displays crumble my resolve
Pull out bigger bag.

Year's first nightingale
Sings in June twilit tree
One more rotation.

Airport to ballpark
Arc of flashing lights to home
Grand Central Parkway

Trackside kiddy park
Lines at twinkling ice cream truck
Cigar by moonlight

Biking Forest Park
Shirtless jocks, strolling aunties
Benches for birdsong.

A century now
Shadowing the avenue
Ascan's giant oaks.

World's best taco truck
Seasoned by soaring Seven
Midnight, Roosevelt.

Surfers' safari
Boardwalk of senior joggers
Slacker Rockaway

Library landing
Tower wall to tower wall
Crossing Queens ferry.

Pichchenda Bao

ODE TO THE BODY RUNNING UNDER THE 7 TRAIN

To the body that does not move
as fast as I want it to
when my son races down
the city sidewalk on his hand-
me-down scooter with its
worn wheels and brakes:
his small figure is getting even
smaller in the distance,
which might not seem
like much,
but even if I run,
I know I won't
catch him.
I think of the marathon
runners pouring over
Queensboro Bridge,
the steady stream of legs
churning onto the streets.
For a moment,
I almost think
I could do it.
Adrenaline making up
for years of neglect.
Then my heart thumps
against my chest,
full of fear
my son won't listen,
won't stop
at the light
to wait for me.
Cars barrel across 43rd Avenue.
My voice doesn't carry.
Oh, heart in my throat.
Oh, flat foot forward.
How fast a little body
moves when they are

unconditionally loved.
How fragile
our fleeting freedom.

TALISMAN FOR A PANDEMIC CHILDHOOD

You are afraid
of their dying
or your dying,
and all the dying
has reduced your world
to the bubble between
Crescent Street and Vernon.
Something unseen hangs in the air,
tugging on the string of mortality
that entangles every touch.
The aftermath is already here
and unimaginable.
The daily sirens doling out grief
at Elmhurst Hospital.
The surges and waves battering
against your fatigue.

You had wanted the whole
world for your children.
You worry what ghosts
will take over their memory.
Remember how their tiny fingers'
first instinct was to hold on
to whoever held them.
They knew nothing
except your density--
your body, their anchor.
Keep kissing them.
Let their soft cheeks yield now
to the steady pressure of love.
Imprint this–
this briefest, deepest pleasure
on their lifelong bodies.

Jared Beloff

VERKLEMPT

After school, I take my daughter to the deli where she tells me
that her class is remembering the Holocaust. I ask
what she is learning. My question lingers at the cheese aisle.
"I don't want to talk about it," she says and for the —th time I am not sure
whether to pry the information or wait and see if there's a
    vocabulary list
for raising your daughter. Her words of the week: *apathy, atrocity*
authoritarian, antisemitism "Why do they hate Jews?"
bigotry, bystander. Someone told her about the Tree of Life
Synagogue in Pittsburgh. We are having trouble defining our *fear*,
or the *hate* lined up and swirling like the wood grain of sleepers
between the rails, *indifferent* as the slats of the pickle barrel in
    front of us.

My daughter's class is remembering the Holocaust.
So, I buy her a bag of pickles and we eat them as we walk home.
She holds them like an ice cream cone, lets the brine fall
between her fingers, smiles at the snap and salt pooling with
    each bite.
We can't speak. Our mouths filled with pleasure.
Our shared silence tastes like *joy.*

COMFORT

At night my daughter runs to our room, scared
the monsters at school will chase her here. Pupils

stretched to drink the darkness as she pulls herself back
to the familiar: this room, cars sighing along Queens boulevard

keeping pace with her breath. *Phew.* It is ok, I promise,
to be afraid. I want to tell her about the long night we spent

at NYU, her jaundiced body, the way her arms shuddered
in the blue light, our reflexes newborn: mine to watch over,

hers to continue growing. We've been measuring each year,
a notch on the kitchen door frame: dates and inches, a reminder

to keep her heels down, to find true form. She wills to expand,
tilts her neck upward as if tracking the sun. The tallest

tree in the city is hidden behind a fence at Alley Pond Park.
A giant tulip requires little maintenance after three centuries of life,

only a policy of "benign neglect." My daughter returns to bed
before I can embrace her, covered up and curling inward already.

Do you think they mind the blanket? She asked once
about the vine-choked trees along Grand Central Parkway,

an illusion of green held close, a child's embrace. *Hush
now.* I realize we are always searching for some kind of comfort.

Francisco Delgado

A QUEENS DAD IN A METS HAT

The 6 o'clock news turns on
us in the form of a neighbor
waving a gun.

We're frozen
in line at the ice cream truck, finished
chatting about the Mets playoff run

just ending. In an instant,
I am one of many:
a Queens dad in a Mets hat

who comes to love
everything more
after it's gone.

Tomorrow on our way
to school, we pass
the Halloween decorations

we've been seeing for weeks.
We laugh a little longer
at the skeletons

and strung-up ghosts. Then
we walk on to celebrate
every day we get to walk on.

THE MERINGUE SKY ABOVE LAGUARDIA

When I first wake up
and it could be
any day of the week,

I wait until it settles
on the right day.
Today,

when there's a plane
flying through the meringue sky
above LaGuardia

and birds have returned
to the trees
outside my window.

I pretend these birds
are the same
that sang to us last year.

And the year before.
And the year before that.

Emily Hockaday

ONLY VESTIGIAL

We see the Polyphemus moth
still as held breath
wings open against the grass

at Maple Grove Cemetery.
My toddler and I lay
beside it, faces pressed

against invisible lines,
the force field of awe.
Today when my mother called—

I was sure
my sister was dead.
She has been moving

toward death and gathering
momentum. Was it only
a week ago

that I scrolled
through her Instagram feed,
counting track marks?

Of the moth,
my child says,
It's dead, right?

I am afraid
to reach out and touch
that large furry body,

and find what I find,
wings as wide
as my spread hand.

Instead a tickle of grass
over those feathered antennae
breaks the spell.

She lifts her forewings first
before hopping into flight.
Later it occurs to me:

this moth was starving to death,
even then, a species whose mouthparts
lead nowhere—are only vestigial.

How long can a body last
unable to take in
nourishment,

running on hunger
and adrenaline
and buried instinct?

SEASONAL WEAR

By noon the fog is lifted, and I am left wondering
if it was ever here. A swarm of stinging flies
rises within me like a cloud. A murmuration

of fears. From the Jackie Robinson the woods
are rows of dark bodies obscured by mist.
Gold crowns the canopy—bright stars fall

from the sweet gum and maple. I brought
myself through the door inside my sternum
and ended up back here, inside out.

It is sweet and sour, the breaking point
I reach. I cry
as the dental hygienist cleans

my teeth. I don't know what snapped
inside me. I tell her mascara
got in my eye: *this is why*

I shouldn't wear makeup. Outside,
the hill is low in the haze. Colorful trees
lay hidden behind, biting hard against

the unfrosted earth. Over the glacial
moraine is Forest Parkway,
and the low land around the bay.
If I prick my ears, I can hear the train.

DeeAnne P. Gorman

SEISMOGRAPHY

There's been a profound
shift
at the base
of my planed existence
upon meeting you
face to face

disrupted emotional tectonic
plates traverse
this way
    and that:
I'm undone
in the most comfortable
at-home sense

the chiropractor
maneuvers my structure
back
into position
and pills swallowed
temporarily calm
a growing inner storm

still   I'm off kilter
and hearing your voice
-- knowing I'll see you
again this earth moves
and I walk through red lights
right into traffic
dazed, confused
but with a purpose:
getting to where you are
sooner
yet   still
not soon enough

There's been a profound
shift
in my core
and I'll never get back
to where I was
before

Erika Meitner

BELL BOULEVARD, 1992

Late-night cicada August I was never asleep
now they call insomnia FOMO, my on-brand
teenage 718 restlessness—what did I keep
of that time? memory a sleight of hand
like an amateur birthday party magician, fire
from a disposable bic to light a blunt warm'd
in a strip-mall parked car hot-boxing desire
some guy's hands in my hair 100% disarm'd
by my unruly curls heat fingers breath by
my boldness, radio playing early perpetual
hip-hop Brand Nubian Tribe EPMD remedy
for our awkward cruising Bell Boulevard thrall
the jolt of summer dancehall hips to prove
how much music in our bodies, if not love

NORTHERN BOULEVARD, 2019

Dinner with Chandra at Little Dumpling where you can't make reservations and she's a vegetarian and they only take cash (I hate that, but whatever) and she says *bereavement group* for self-care's sake, for her panic attacks at work, and the first night she went it was state-of-emergency torrential quarter-sized hail, water pouring—let it come, the signal problems, sheets of rain swamping subway platforms, sweet drowning. First her mom had trouble breathing, then a sense of doom and died so fast: 30 days after the ovarian cancer diagnosis. We greet our server, order, try to remember names of anyone we liked by the end of high school and come up blank. The lease on her Chevy is up in a day so we drive Northern Boulevard on a weeknight past my dope-fiend ex's apartment, past Café Oasis where we'd patio smoke. I've been away so long, haven't cruised Northern in 20 years, roll the window, throw the radio on Hot 97, pass White Castle and Carvel, whisper *I miss you*.

Hila Ratzabi

REDWOOD

Our twelve-year-old legs dangle limb to limb
from the tree in Cunningham Park
that stands not much bigger
than our growing bodies.
We write dreams and plans in a notebook:
a farm, a kibbutz, an elsewhere.

Anatte rides horses at Lynne's School in Forest Hills
every Wednesday afternoon, galloping
from finitude. We search for spells
in books of Irish myths and kabbalah
spread out on the pink carpet
of my bedroom floor. We believe
we can stop time as it taps
windy fingers on our shoulders.

Anatte tells me you can't pronounce
God's name: it's all breath. *Try it.*
I try. I stop trying. We're forty-one.
She stops riding horses—*too dangerous a sport*,
she says—not knowing
that Arthur Cunningham, namesake
of our park, died in a riding accident
on Redwood, a horse
for whom the renovated playground
is named like a warning.

Redwood: a tree found nowhere
near Queens, except the one we saw
on a school trip to the Museum of Natural History,
cross-section of a giant sequoia towering
over our heads—fourteen hundred years old, *older
than the English language*, our teacher said
as she pointed to the dates on the wood,
one label for each century,
history pinned to its rings.

Just yesterday at dinner my kid said
he doesn't want to be a grown-up—
too scary, too serious. What
can I say? We wrote
our petitions. We asked the ancients
to give up their secrets. We mouthed
the Holy Name, circled the Tree of Life
with our tightly held pens,
wrote the future, crossed it out,
consulted the old books. The tree
that held us is long gone,
cut down before I could return
to learn its name.

Vijay R. Nathan

WHERE MY ORIGINAL FACE BEFORE I WAS BORN EMERGES

A breeze scattered the manuscript *Translate this Sweetness*
I don't know the importance of those drafts of poems
While the birds move outside, Tabby monitors them
The gray Buddha holds silent watch over the patio

I don't know the importance of those drafts of poems
My friends start a new thread and the alert is no longer silent
The gray Buddha holds silent watch over the patio
And the heatwaves continues in Rockaway Park, NYC

My friends start a new thread and the alert is no longer silent
The memory of her breaking her pencil returns
And the heatwaves continues in Rockaway Park, NYC
My internal monologue submerges into the fertile void

The memory of her breaking her pencil returns
I prefer to meditate with a soft gaze, never closed eyes
My internal monologue submerges into the fertile void
I have never seen the the Sun acknowledge the Moon's smile

I prefer to meditate with a soft gaze, never closed eyes
NYC Parks department is building Rockaway Beach 14 new groins
I have never seen the the Sun acknowledge the Moon's smile
The turbulent tides, controlled by that celestial tension, is receding

NYC Parks department is building Rockaway Beach 14 new groins
A breeze scattered the manuscript *Translate this Sweetness*
The turbulent tides, controlled by that celestial tension, is receding
While the birds move outside, Tabby monitors them

Richard Jeffrey Newman

ACCOUNTABILITY

Walking home in the streetlamp dark,
the neighborhood quiet except for the cars
playing Red-Light-Green-Light
east and west on 35th Avenue,
I swing higher than I should
the canvas bag I'm carrying
and a sharp tension pulls tight
the muscle running down the edge
of my right shoulder blade,
echo of the briefcase
heavier than it should be
that I carry daily from class to class.

I stop on the corner of 78th Street,
stretch the tightness out,
decide I need a walk home
long enough to let the day I've had
unwind whatever path within me
will bring it to a place of rest,
and turn right instead of left, and then
at Roosevelt Avenue, turn right again.
Above my head, the number 7 train
beats a rhythm I could write a poem to,
and I should write a poem, I think,
filled as I still am
with what that young poet
new to the open mic
asked the group of us
sipping our final cups
before the café closed for the night.

"Why," she leaned forward,
watching me from the corner of her eye,
"can't we just let poems exist
without judging them?" I thought
of the colleague who over the years

has made sure each of the twelve books
he's published in English
sits on my shelf;
how I've only finished the first two,
leaving the rest with a dog-eared page
to mark the poem where his speaker
becomes the guy at the bar
with only two stories to tell
and not enough sense to know
it doesn't matter how well he tells them:
he's told them far too many times already.

He sat ramrod straight
earlier this week
at the conference table
empty except for the evidence
gathered against him—memos,
observations, formal complaints,
all neatly stacked in the center,
waiting for our department chair
to lead him yet one more time
through the sequence of events
he still insisted on his right
to defend himself against.

"It appears," he started, but then,
as it had done three times before,
the fog he refused to admit
he could not stop
in its spread across his memory
asserted itself, blocking his way
to the words that should have come next.
He turned in a silence
I know he did not choose
to each of us, one by one,
eyes brimming with the loss
he could no longer pretend
he was not suffering,
and when his gaze met mine
I felt his shame
as if it were my own:

he could no longer
find his way to poetry either.

"We should," that young woman's voice
comes back to me as I cross the empty square
where 73rd Street and Broadway meet,
"be lifting each other up, not
creating hierarchies of worth."
I wanted that morning nothing more
than to lift my colleague up,
to be for him not just his union representative,
but someone whose love
could help him love
all that was failing within him.

"Remember," he put his hand on my arm
as the meeting ended
and I lifted my briefcase
filled almost to bursting
with the graded essays
my students were waiting for,
"if you presume to publish,
public accountability
comes with the package.
Friendship has nothing to do with it!"
He searched my face
as if he did not know who I was,
or as if he wanted me
to tell him who he was.
"Own your failures," he whispered.

I stop on the overpass above the BQE,
watch the northbound cars
coming up the exit ramp
that when I was a kid was red cobblestone
and the traffic light that's still there,
and the congestion there always was,
granted us a few more minutes together
when my father brought me and my brother
back from his parents' place in Boro Park.

My brother is long dead; my father
is dying each day less and less slowly.
I try to imagine the time he has left
as a distance between us
we still have a chance to close,
but what I remember
is standing with him
while my wife helped our son
browse the children's section
of the Union Square Barnes & Noble
and handing him a Holocaust anthology
opened to the pages where my poems appeared.
He smiled to see my name in print,
glanced left to right, right to left,
then pulled open one side
of his gray London Fog trench coat.
"If I were a younger man, Richard,"
he smiled, cocking his head,
pointing with his eyes
and with the hand that held the book
to the inside pocket where that sentence ended.
All these years later, and I still don't know
what he wanted that gesture to mean,
but now, as I head north on 69th Street,
trailing behind me the sadness
that I won't miss him when he's gone,
I'm glad he was not that younger man,
that after I put *Beyond Lament*
back where I found it,
he never mentioned my writing again,
not even to ask,
as my colleague did
every time he saw me,
even this afternoon,
as he paced the parking lot
behind our offices,
pipe in his left hand,
his right reaching for mine,
as if he were not waiting
for his daughter to take him
to where he would start

the life he had left, as if instead
he was greeting an old friend
he called by a name that was not mine,
and the only thing that mattered
was what had always mattered between us:
"What are you working on these days?"

Anda Totoreanu

THANK YOU

in the style of Ross Gay

In my fifth floor New York walk-up
guest-room/office
I look out into the courtyard
see cherry blossoms against grey bricks,
finches chirping,
& the angry mother in the window
across from mine
yelling at her kids - maybe reminding them
to pick up their clothes

blues and pinks begin to paint the sky - a canvas
above the grey, soot-covered apartments

I won't leave my tower today -
instead looking down from above at the kingdom
left to the squirrels and the jesting birds

I close my eyes, bring my hands
to the heart of my forehead,
bowing with gratitude -
Thank you, *thank you.*

TOMORROW

I'm sick of hiding from the air

do you remember what it's like
to sing in a cathedral full of people,
your voice weaving among the many

to walk through the Cloisters
feeling the cool tile beneath as you journey back in time
discovering medieval life through strange unicorn tapestries

do you remember what it's like
to sweat & let your limbs freely roam
on a dance floor somewhere in Chinatown
finding their own narrative,
their own place in the world

to hear Barry Harris play at the Village Vanguard
smoky notes heavy in the air

do you remember what it's like
to have your belly rumble with laughter,
trying to keep sangria from spraying out your nose

We've been playing the song at its lowest volume.
We've been holding our breath.

Micah Zevin

THE CHEAP, THE VERSATILE AND THE ENEMIES OF THE OVERINFLATED

If you burn off your fingerprints, do you even exist?
Can you play the upright bass or are you a shadowy ghoul,
Everyone's stool pigeon, inhabiting the rarefied air of a
Switzerland type nation, hard to identify, spare in autobiographical
details, but not masks, when branding with overpriced overinflated
milk, eggs, ham, tortas grilled/fried wafting from *Super Star Farm* bodegas.
Are you surprised you can buy human eyes on consignment but coffees prices,
over the counter cough medicines, lettuce keep fluctuating, sky
rocketing at all Jackson Heights *Trade Fairs*, *Key Foods*. After explosions,
transcending, stunning vignettes, anxious at old economic frauds predicting
our demise on the back of, or as the fault of the working class, not boney
horny warlocks with less than secret insider tricks. How long will the weed
grow untended? After smoking, do we drink a glass of Malbec or Pinot Noir,
and complain, scour the salt vinegar chip bag half filled with air?

1/25/2021: PUTTING OUT THE FIRES

As I was running errands at the pharmacy,
and grocery store yesterday, it was getting colder
and colder on Northern Blvd; I even noticed a frozen river
puddle of water underneath a parked car. Nature has a kind of
magic slow or fast and deliberate but definitely not a
snake-oil sales (person) (usually men) just sometimes predictable/
unpredictable through analysis of dates by our weather people.
My wife had a craving for spicy food last night
We ordered from a fusion Tibetan restaurant called OM Wok.
My wife got the Szechuan shrimp drowning in red peppers
and Szechuan peppercorns, and it was so hot it was difficult to
swallow as our eyes watered, and we down one glass after another,
followed by rice, rice, rice, and thank the heavens for butter tea so
yummy smooth. This morning while sleeping deeply in the shaded
sunshine of our living room, I am on fire, twisted stomach muscles,
congested, insides stinging inside and out until dizzy, dreams of
swimming away from the river of spice I love but haven't eaten much
of or been able to handle this past pandemic year. What I need is health,
no cares, right? Some self-maintenance, not magic but hearty, peeling off
old layers until new skin arises hopefully glowing as the body
becomes limber
and is up-lifted.

Linda Kleinbub

SITTING ON THE BLEACHERS OF JUNIPER VALLEY PARK

Wind blows through me
pulls my hair to cover my eyes.
Left of me
roller-skating boys smack hockey sticks,
bikers fly by.

Baseball field before me
the pitcher's mound has worn to the ground.
Empty field is a quiet sound
a muffle of voices
a distant rumble of motorbikes.

Wind continues to play with my hair.
Wind blows through me.
Overhead the peach leaves
shush with wind.

Who's wiser?
Peach tree next to me
will probably live longer.
Knows how to survive
swaying in sunshine.

Relaxes deep down into her roots
holds firmly to the earth
allows herself to be fed
by the grace of rain.

Peach tree, teach me how to live
keep me planted
swaying in the sunshine.
Wind blows through me.
I listen
planted
grow.

Rob Ostrom

THE ANTEDILUVIAN HORNET'S NEST BEGINS TO THAW

in this world the seats are taken and people
are fighting about one thing when really
they're angry about oceans their mothers
the buildings here were built out of altitude
and envy we use umbrellas to slow our fall
every day we wake with jeans on and what
isn't lost in us belongs to someone else
the armchair where a resident died the line
outside a bar rain on the car roof the taxi
driver's near-silent breath all you've ever seen
of him are eyes in a rearview mirror
and as long as the noises and the quarter
wits and the old boots and mark my words
the dogs have gotten fatter with neglect
and the football teams on the Astroturf their
cleats the sound of a hollow field like the sounds
under your bed where the machete's kept there's
a troublemaker who doesn't belong in this poem
the problem of love here too a scraping sound
a rattling muffler one day a dream like rage will
seep into your waking life you might be eating
a mooncake on the subway or saying a prayer
without posture and the next thing you know
your head rolls back the way a houseplant bends
toward whatever keeps it blooming you won't
notice the dirt in your nails or that you have
devastated everything in your path your skeleton
talks to the pottery now the studs in the wall
the chipped glass and even though you don't have
work the alarm clock which belongs to someone
who left you still wakes you at seven in the morning

THE BEAR WRESTLER

makes me wait in the car outside my girlfriend's house
sitting beside me in his wool overcoat
he's searching his pockets for a Fisherman's Friend
he calls them breath mints
he is his wool overcoat pockets full of leaves
he is his wool overcoat pockets full
of Fisherman's Friends buried in pipe tobacco loose change
he'll find me two dirty lozenges one for now and one for
his wool overcoat is dry grass under snow-wet leaves
he is his wool overcoat is a grainfield he wraps around me
he empties his pockets a ring falls out
then a house then a family
his overcoat contains everyone of him
he says let's build ourselves a fire

McCaela Prentice

DIFFERENT FLOODS

I saw news last night that worried me.

someone asks about the flood, and we all mention different ones.

my neighbor waters my scotch bonnets when I'm not home.
I move them out of reach. someone suggests retaliation but we
are thinking again of different floods.

when I walk home and see them red up on my balcony,
I think it's something of a miracle. like cheesecloth
in my drawer or Ample Hills reopening.

floods, actually, cleanse nothing. up north
a grocery store has aisles of mud. people dance
in the high water and microbiologists weep.

it's some miracle the rain doesn't break this heat.
another that we don't flood the streets.
all of this miraculous inaction.

all of this news that worries me.

I ask about the forest fire, and you mention a different one.

Jared Harél

RAT WARS

When restaurants shuttered
and commuters cleared the streets,

our borough's well-fed rat population
starved, grew angry, cannibalistic,

waged rat wars against neighboring
rat territories with which they'd coexisted,

rather peacefully, for years.
Moreover, more rats were spotted

in daylight, racing in packs
down barren sidewalks while behind

our human windows, balconies
and screens, we watched

their armies nose forward in protest
over a bargain broken without

ever knowing it: scraps for silence.
Half-eaten hoagies for which they'd go

underground, scurry in darkness,
in a word: disappear. But now

rats were coming. The rats were here,
while always in deep cracks

and choked gutters, epics
unfurled beneath grander-scale

dramas—bodies hurled on bodies
in celebration or defeat.

THE CLOSING

The checks have cleared.
Everything is signed.
Your new lawn forests
like a greedy hand.
The Recreation Dept.
requires proof of residency
to issue passes
to the village pool.
Nothing is so different
or beyond repair.
You need food and shelter.
Reliable internet
and a night dark with stars.
You own a garage clicker.
The bank owns your throat.
Not a single neighbor
can pronounce
your name.

BIOS

Pichchenda Bao is a Cambodian American poet and writer. Her work has been featured in numerous publications, exhibitions, and events. She is co-editor, with Nicole Callihan and Jennifer Franklin, of the anthology, *Braving the Body* (Harbor Editions). She has received fellowships and support from Aspen Words, Kundiman, Bethany Arts Community, and Queens Council on the Arts. She lives, writes and raises her three children in New York City. More at www.pichchendabao.com.

Jared Beloff is the author of *Who Will Cradle Your Head* (ELJ Editions, 2023) and the editor of the MCU poetry anthology, *Marvelous Verses* (Daily Drunk, 2021). His work can be found at *AGNI, Baltimore Review, Image Journal, Terrain.com* and elsewhere. He is a Poetry Editor at *The Weight Journal* and Managing Editor of *Porcupine Literary*. You can find him on his website www.jaredbeloff.com. He is a teacher who lives in Forest Hills with his wife and two daughters.

Francisco Delgado is an Assistant Professor of English at BMCC (CUNY). He is the author of *Adolescence, Secondhand* (Honeysuckle Press, 2018), and his poems have recently appeared in *JMWW, Rejection Letters*, and *Lost Balloon* and are often set in Queens, New York, where he lives with his wife and their son.

Sherese Francis (she/they) describes themselves as an AlkyMist of the I-Magination, finding expression through poetry, interdisciplinary arts (collage, book and paper arts, sound and performance art, text art), workshop facilitation, editing, and literary curation. Her(e) work takes inspiration from her(e) Afro-Caribbean heritage (Barbados and Dominica), and studies in Afrofuturism and Black Speculative Arts, mythology and etymology. Sherese has published work in various journals and magazines, and published four chapbooks, *Lucy's Bone Scrolls, Variations on Sett/ling Seed/ling, Recycling a Why That Rules Over My Sacred Sight,* and *Lady Liberty Smashing Stones.*

Trace Howard DePass is the author of *self-portrait as the space between us* (PANK 2018) & *BOOTless* (Diode Editions 2024). His work has been featured with *Poetry Foundation, Ours Poetica*, NPR's *The Takeaway, SAND, Entropy, Split This Rock, Poetry Project, Bettering American Poetry*, and the Academy of American Poets Poem-a-Day series. DePass is a fellow with Poets House, Obsidian, and Teachers & Writers.

DeeAnne P. Gorman has been a featured poet in the U.S. and France, with work appearing in *The Sunday Independent* (Ashland, KY), *The Casanova Quarterly* (Washington, DC & NYC), *Servi Bleu* (France), *Upstairs at Duroc* (Paris), *West Side Arts Coalition Newsletter*, and Riverside Poets' and Parkside Poets' annual anthologies (NYC). Awards include John Rolfe Middle School's Poetry Prize (Richmond, VA), and the Molly Bloom Poetry Competition of Paris (1999) 2nd Place. She initiated Greater Astoria Historical Society's "April is National Poetry Month" event, now in its eighth year. Her own poetry collection, *Document*, came out with NoNet Press in 2018.

Jared Harél is the author, most recently, of *Let Our Bodies Change the Subject* (University of Nebraska Press, 2023) which was selected by Kwame Dawes as the Winner of the Prairie Schooner Raz/Shumaker Book Prize in Poetry and was named a Finalist for the Paterson Poetry Prize and the National Jewish Book Award. For more information, visit: jaredharel.com

Emily Hockaday is the author of *In a Body* (Harbor Editions 2023), *Naming the Ghost* (Cornerstone Press 2022), and six chapbooks. She is a De Groot Foundation Writer of Note and a Café Royal Cultural Foundation, NY City Artist Corps, and NYFA Queens Art Fund recipient. Her poems have appeared in numerous literary journals in print and online, including *Electric Literature* and the *North American Review.* She is the editor of *Heartbeat of the Universe* (Interstellar Flight Press 2024). Emily writes about ecology, parenthood, the urban environment, and chronic illness. She can be found online at www.emilyhockaday.com and @E_Hockaday.

The former Queens Borough Poet Laureate (2010-2014), **Paolo Javier**'s work has featured in PS1 MoMA's Greater NY and in Queens International. His most recent book, *True Account of Talking to the 7 in Sunnyside (*Roof Books), was a finalist for the 2022 Big Other Book Award for Poetry. He lives in Jackson Heights, Queens.

Olena Jennings is the author of the poetry collection *The Age of Secrets* (Lost Horse Press, 2022) and the novel *Temporary Shelter* (Cervena Barva Press, 2021). She is a translator of collections by Ukrainian poets, Kateryna Kalytko, together with Oksana Lutsyshyna, Iryna Shuvalova, together with the author, and Vasyl Makhno. Her translation, together with the author, of Yuliya Musakovska's *The God of Freedom* was released in May 2024 from Arrowsmith Press. She founded and curates the Poets of Queens reading series and press.

Robert Kaplan is the author of *"Past/Present" and Other Poems*, published in September 2023 by Poets of Queens Press. He has an MFA in Creative Writing from the University of Arizona, a PhD in Early American Literature from the CUNY Graduate Center, and teaches expository writing at Stony Brook University. His poetry has appeared in *KGB Lit* and, in a former life, in numerous small literary magazines that no longer exist. He is currently at work on two manuscripts: one a collection of unfinished and finished older and newer poems, and the other a book-length poem about being an eldercaregiver.

Linda Kleinbub is the founding editor of Pink Trees Press, curator of Fahrenheit Open Mic, contributing editor at Girls Write Now, and co-founder of Pen Pal Poets. Her first book of poetry is *Cover Charge* (Autonomedia, 2022.) She's co-editor of *Silver Tongued Devil Anthology* (Pink Trees Press, 2020.) Linda was one of six local poets invited to read at the Americas Poetry Festival of New York 2021. She earned her MFA at The New School. She's been published in *Best American Poetry, Brooklyn Rail, Observer, Yahoo! Life, First Literary Review East, Sensitive Skin*, and *LiveMag!* She is a native New Yorker.

Ananda Lima is the author of *Craft: Stories I Wrote for the Devil* (Tor Books, 2024), and *Mother/land* (Black Lawrence Press, 2021, winner of the Hudson Prize). Her work has appeared in four chapbooks, including Amblyopia (Bull City Press), and publications such as *The American Poetry Review, Poets.org, Kenyon Review Online, Gulf Coast, Witness,* and elsewhere. She has served as a mentor at the New York Foundation for the Arts (NYFA) Immigrant Artist Program and currently serves as a contributing editor for *Poets & Writers.* Originally from Brazil, she lived in Queens, and now lives in Chicago.

Maria Lisella's collections include: *Thieves in the Family* (NYQ Books), *Amore on Hope Street* (Finishing Line Press) and *Two Naked Feet* (Poets Wear Prada). Her newest collection, *The Man with a Plan* is pending publication. Featured on The Poet and the Poem at the Library of Congress, she is the sixth Queens Poet Laureate, and an Academy of American Poets Fellow. She co-curates the Italian American Writers Association readings, leads workshops for underserved communities, is a travel journalist, and Poetry Editor for Voices in Italian Americana.

Erika Meitner is the author of six books of poems, including *Useful Junk* (BOA Editions, 2022), and *Holy Moly Carry Me* (BOA Editions, 2018)--winner of the 2018 National Jewish Book Award and a finalist for the National Book Critics Circle Award in poetry. Her poems have been published most recently in *Electric Literature, Oxford American, The New Yorker, Orion, The New Republic, Virginia Quarterly Review,* and *The Rumpus*. Meitner is currently a professor of English and MFA program director at the University of Wisconsin-Madison. She was born and raised in Queens. You can find more about her at erikameitner.com.

Vijay R. Nathan published "Escape from Samsara" (2016) and "Celebrity Sadhana, Or How to Meditate with a Hammer" (2018) and was published by Poets of Queens for "Breakdown Dancer" (2021). He's a two time Masters degree winner with an MLS from St. John's and a Masters in Clinical Mental Health Counseling from Naropa University. He's NYC native son of Indian immigrants who love all religions so they sent him to a Catholic school. So he loves Jesus, Vishnu, and Buddha.

Richard Jeffrey Newman has published three books of his own poetry, *T'shuvah* (Fernwood Press 2023), *Words for What Those Men Have Done* (Guernica Editions 2017) and *The Silence of Men* (CavanKerry Press 2006), as well as three books of translation from classical Persian poetry, *Selections from Saadi's Gulistan, Selections from Saadi's Bustan* (Global Scholarly Publications 2004 & 2006) and *The Teller of Tales: Stories from Ferdowsi's Shahameh* (Junction Press 2011). He curates the First Tuesdays reading series in Jackson Heights, NY and is in his 35th year as Professor of English and Creative Writing at Nassau Community College. His website is www.richardjnewman.com.

Robert Ostrom's latest collection, *The Bear Wrestler,* will be published by Saturnalia Books in Spring 2025. He lives in Ridgewood and teaches at New York City College of Technology.

McCaela Prentice (she/her) is living and writing in Astoria, NY. She is thinking about what pepper varieties to plant in her garden this year. Her poems have previously appeared in *HAD*, *Ghost City Review*, and *Denver Quarterly*. Her first poetry collection *"JUNK DRAWER HEART"* was published in 2020 with Invisible Hand Press.

Hila Ratzabi is the author of *There Are Still Woods* (June Road Press, 2022), which won a gold Nautilus Book Award and was a finalist for a National Indie Excellence Award. Her poetry has been published widely in literary journals, including *Narrative, Linebreak, Alaska Quarterly Review, The Adroit Journal*, and others, and in *The Bloomsbury Anthology of Contemporary Jewish American Poetry* and *Ghost Fishing: An Eco-Justice Poetry Anthology*. She holds an MFA in Poetry from Sarah Lawrence College (2007). She lives outside Chicago.

Anda Totoreanu is a Romanian-American immigrant, poet, lawyer, choral singer, and lover of all things outdoors. Her poems have been published by *The Poetry Society of New York*, *Pandemic Poems*, *Gravel Literary Journal*, and on *The Song Is...* blog. Her work has also been published in several legal and academic journals on immigration, minority rights and conflict resolution. Anda's poetry explores love, loss, vulnerability, coming to terms with your past, living in the present, and the peace of finding yourself in nature. She received her creative writing minor from Lafayette College. You may find many of her poems at www.instagram.com/poemsbyanda/.

Bruce E. Whitacre

Good Housekeeping, Poets Wear Prada, is a BookLife Reviews Editors Pick. *The Elk in the Glade: The World of Pioneer and Painter Jennie Hicks*, placed 2nd in Contemporary Poetry at The BookFest Spring 2023. His crown sonnet about the culture of violence won the Nebraska Poetry Society's 2023 Open Poetry Contest. He has been published in Queensbound and many anthologies and journals. "Leave Meeting" is included in Diane Lockward's craft book, *The Strategic Poet*, Terrapin Books, 2021. Nominated for Pushcart and Best of the Net. He lives with his husband in Forest Hills, NY. www.brucewhitacre.com.

Micah Zevin is a librarian poet living in Jackson Heights, Queens, N.Y. He has published articles and poems most recently at the *Heavy Feather Review*, *Big Other*, *The Bowery Gothic*, *The Poets of Queens Anthology*, *Narrative Northeast*, *Pine Hills Review*, *Spoke Journal*, *Fence*, *First Literary Review East*, *Brevitas* 20-2023 Anthology of the Short Poem and the Queensbound poetry project. His first book of poems, *Metal, Heavy* was published December 1st, 2020 from Olena Jennings and Poets of Queens Press. He created/curates an open mic/poetry prompt workshop called The Risk of Discovery Reading Series.